A Century of Music in Jersey 1890-1990

CHAS. E. LARBALESTIER

To my wife

If music be the food of love –
play on

Shakespeare

ISBN 0 9516736 0 2

Designed, printed and bound
by Islandprint, Jersey

Contents

Introduction

This is not a book about the many musicians that have visited our shores. Over the years we have had some of the top musicians in their field. This is the story of the people who have made an impression on music in Jersey and continue to do so.

I have used photographs to tell the story of music in Jersey, as I felt that this was the best medium to capture the changing style, instrumentation and fashion; also one can immediately identify with photographs.

Sadly I have not been able to include all the various people who have contributed so much to music in Jersey – for example, the fine choirs, organists and the hard working teachers – this is beyond the scope of this book.

I would like to dedicate this book to all the musicians, both professional and amateur, who have devoted their time and talent to the enjoyment of others.

Chas. E. Larbalestier
6th June 1990

CHAPTER ONE

The Early Years

The latter part of the nineteenth century was an interesting period for music. People were now beginning to reap the benefit of the industrial revolution; more people could afford to go on holiday and wanted to be entertained. Even before the end of the century Jersey was a holiday resort and holiday makers could find plenty of entertainment at places like "West Park Pavilion", "Springfield" and the "Theatre Royal". If one could not afford these places, the military bands would provide free concerts at the various bandstands or, if the weather was bad, at the nearest convenient venue.

The year 1902 saw the coronation of Edward VII, and as can be imagined there was plenty of call on the bands. Apart from the three Militia bands, there was the band of the "Devonshire Regiment" that was stationed at Fort Regent.

As well as military bands, vaudeville acts were being booked to appear in Jersey. Some of these included a large amount of music in their acts, like "The White Coons", "The Behans" and later "The Gaieties".

There were four main music shops, "E. Lee's" in New Street, "Milnes" in Halkett Place, "Donaldson Brothers" on the corner of Belmont Road and "McKee's" then situated in Bath Street.

The "Concours Musical" took place in 1906 and 1907. Bands came from all over France to compete in this event, in the true spirit of "Entente Cordiale". These events were so successful that one wonders why they were not continued.

During this time the "Jersey Musical Union" was formed. Right from the start they were so popular that they were able to send a band to France every year, so extending the "Entente Cordiale". This happy state of affairs lasted until the outbreak of World War I.

Jersey Museum Services

On January 17th 1890 the Cecilian Orchestral Society was inaugurated. Their conductor was C. E. R. Stevens. The orchestra took its name from the day of their first concert on November 22nd 1889, which was St Cecilia's Day. Note the little girl looking out of the top window.

Jersey Museum Services

Here we have a photograph of an all ladies orchestra taken c.1891. The venue is thought to be the old West Park Pavilion, known locally as "The Tin House". It is known today as the "Inn on the Park". Note the gas lighting for the stage illumination.

The McKee family has long been associated with music in Jersey. Many will remember their music shop in Beresford Street. Here we have a photograph of the McKee family taken c.1892. On the left of the photograph is Adolphus McKee; he was bandmaster of the 1st or West Regimental Band of the Royal Jersey Militia. Next to him is Lily McKee, she played the piano. Next to her is Mother, then George McKee on bass. Seated in the front is Frederick McKee, violin, his elder brother Adolphus McKee (Junior), and Henry McKee who doubled 'cello and trombone. History does not record what the name of the dog was. It is not thought that he was the model for "His Master's Voice".

F. McK

I could not resist this charming photograph of these little girls. It has been suggested that the house in the background was the old convent in David Place, c.1894. The girls are playing between them six violins, a zither, an autoharp, a mandolin, a guitar and a banjo. Presumably the two girls without instruments were the singers.

Auth

Jersey Museum Services

The Northamptonshire Regiment replaced the Yorkshires in 1895. Here is the Northamptonshire Band at Fort Regent. The small dog in the foreground is probably the regimental mascot. An interesting point is that the band has two double-bass players and two brass bass players.

Jersey Museum Services

This is a superb photograph of the fife and drum band of the 2nd or East Regiment of the Royal Jersey Light Infantry, c.1896. On the bass drum can be seen the battle honour "1781" awarded to the Royal Jersey Militia by Queen Victoria in 1881 for their part in the Battle of Jersey.

Although he is not strictly a musician, I could not resist this postcard c.1901. Could he perhaps be Jersey's first disc jockey?

Auth

Edmund Bosanquet,
THE JERSEY VIOLINIST,
MUSICAL DIRECTOR,
ALHAMBRA, BLACKPOOL,
In his original and unique Selections and masterly renderings (with specially illustrated effects) of Violin Solos by the great masters, performed by PAGANINI, DR. JOACHIM, SARASATE, KUBELIK, etc.—a revelation.

8/2/1903

How are you getting on with your practising & Hamburg, shall send in your name on Wednesday.
Sincerely yrs.
L. J. Baker

Author

Edmund Bosanquet was a not Jersey violinist. In 1902 he gave recital at the Opera House and t following year he left Jersey to take his appointment at the Alhamb Blackpool.

Author

Author

The "White Coon" Banjo Team played the Opera House for three seasons. In 1904 they took part in the Battle of the Flowers.

Did they really allow "buskers" in St Helier in 1904?

A May

History does not record how proficient or otherwise Harry the Guide was on the banjo but I feel he may have had some musical talent; he certainly had a very professional approach to all the other aspects of entertaining our tourists.

Graham Harris

Author

Here is a postcard of the Band of the East Surrey's taken on the New North Quay. This photograph was produced in 1905 by the great French photographer Louis Levy.

Author

Salvation Army Bands have always been noted for their good musicians and I am sure that this band was no exception. Here they are in 1906 where the old Weighbridge used to stand, at the top of the New North Quay.

This is one of the French bands that took part in the "Concours Musical de Jersey" in 1907. This was the band from Breuil. Below is a card advertising the event and the "Entente Cordiale".

A. May

Author

Author

Author

This is the Jersey Musical Union taken at The Chalet Hotel, Pontac, in 1908. The hotel was well-known as a tourist resort and throughout the summer they would have concerts there. Other attractions were the gardens, a maze and a bandstand. The hotel is now known as La Fontaine.

Auth

Auth

These two photographs show a subtle sense of humour. With and without their hats. One wonders what prompted them to have these photographs taken. If only one could hear a record or a tape of this brass band . . .

Author

This orchestra was partly made up of the boys of the "Sacré Coeur" Orphanage at Summerland, Rouge Bouillon. This photograph in fact is taken looking to the right of the orphanage, c.1909.

Author

The Boys' Brigade, 4th Jersey Company. Here we have the boys of the St James' Brigade in 1910. One wonders how many survived the First World War.

"The Gaieties" as they appeared in 1913. They were well-known in Jersey, coming back year after year, when they would perform at various venues including "West Park Pavilion" or, as it was known, "The Tin House".

Auth

The bandstand in the Triangle Park, c.1910. What a pleasant way to spend an afternoon, listening to the band. If the weather was inclement the band would play in the nearby West Park Pavilion. Today a statue of Queen Victoria stands where the bandstand used to be.

Graham Har

Graham Harris

It is a little surprising how popular ladies' orchestras were at the turn of the century. I have found reference to this one in 1913, when they played at West Park Pavilion, but I think this photograph is perhaps earlier.

Author

Here is an excellent photograph of the Jersey Musical Union taken at the Foire de Caen in 1913. As can be seen they had now acquired uniforms. In the centre is the bandleader Mr Brunt, and his daughter is on his right. On his left is the President, Mr Pérédès, and the Mayor of Caen. The young piccolo player next to the bass drum is George Pinel. I met Mr Pinel in 1987 when he was a very young eighty-nine years old.

CHAPTER TWO

Music and Dancing

After the end of the war people were once again able to relax and enjoy themselves. The tourism business was booming as never before and with it the demand for music and entertainment. In 1921 we had the visit of King George V and his charming Queen, and as usual the Jersey Musical Union was called on to perform much of the music.

The following year P. G. Larbalestier was accepted by the British Music Society, and the same year saw the inauguration of the Jersey Symphony Orchestra under his baton.

On the popular music front, "Dixieland Jazz" along with the "Charleston" and the "Black Bottom" had swept across America to Great Britain and then to Jersey. At the West Park Pavilion the "Gaieties" were appearing and dance bands were to be enjoyed at most of the hotels.

It was during the nineteen-thirties that the dance bands came into their own. West Park Pavilion had been purpose-built to cater for dancing. It replaced the old "Tin House" as it was called, and offered one of the best dance floors in the Island. When it opened in 1931, the first band was called "The Pavilion Players". The following year they performed for the first time their own composition "Isle of Dreams".

Many of the residential hotels were employing dance bands. The Aberfeldy, Hotel de l'Europe and the Imperial were just a few. Most of the smaller bands consisted of five or six musicians and the general standard of music was high.

In 1935 the "Forum Cinema" opened. Edward O'Henry played the big Compton organ to entertain the patrons. Although the Forum was not a venue for bands or orchestras at that time, in later years it was to be home to all sorts of music and variety.

Although back in the 'twenties there had been "Dixieland Jazz", a new form of music was beginning to be heard. This came to be called "Modern Jazz". Some of the musicians were fine jazz players. Tommy Arnold's band was at the "Plaza Ballroom" and they were adept at this new form of music.

So it was that Jersey was a wonderful place to come on holiday. Hotels were fairly inexpensive, cigarettes and drink were cheap and every night one could go dancing to some of the best small bands in Britain. And then came World War II.

JEP

The inauguration of the "Jersey Symphony Orchestra" took place in 1922. The conductor was P. G. Larbalestier and the leader Walter Larbalestier. This photograph was taken some years after the orchestra was formed, but the personnel were essentially the same.

This is the "Jesters Dance Band" in 1924. A typical line-up of the time. This was the hey–day of the "Black Bottom" and the "Charleston".

Aut

Another typical dance band, "The Scarlet Band", they played at the "Hotel de l'Europe" in 1927.

Auth

M. Harper

This was the "Gloucester Dance Band" in 1929. They took their name from the Gloucester Hotel where they were the resident band. In the original line-up was Maurice Harper trumpet, Dick Troy violin, Alf Bowerman banjo, George Tierney piano, and Billy Stephens drums. George Tierney was later replaced by Maud Glendewar on piano, a popular musician during the Occupation.

David Jones

Another typical dance band of the period, c.1933. This quartette played the Fairbanks Hotel, now called Anneport Bay Hotel.

Auth

This is the Royal Jersey Militia Band in 1930. The photograph was taken at the old Town Arsenal which now houses the Police and the Firemen.

Author

Author

This is the "New Pavilion" when it opened in 1931. This fine building replaced a rather primitive building known locally as "The Tin Hut". For a short time the name was changed to "Behans" and then it became "The Inn on the Park". In 1988 it was extensively and beautifully renovated. Jersey can well be proud of the old "Pav".

David Jc

Aut

An all-girl band playing at St Helier House Hotel c.1932. The hotel was situated in La Motte Street and in later years came to be known as The Imperial Hotel.

W. Stephens

The "Gloucester Hotel" was situated in Gloucester Street next to the "Chelsea Hotel". Later it was incorporated in with the "Hotel Angleterre". In 1932 the resident band was the "Gloucester Dance Ensemble". On clarinet and saxophones was Jimmy Foot, Bobby Le Riche was on violin, Maud Glendewar piano and Billy Stephens drums. Notice how narrow the bass drum is.

Author

This is the "Gloucester Dance Band" at the "Mayfair Hotel" in 1933. Except for Arthur Baudin on piano, it was the same line-up as the previous year. What makes this photograph of more than passing interest is the large cone-shaped object in the foreground. It was called a sub-clarinet. It's function was to change the tone of the clarinet, much in the way that a mute does with a trumpet. One would put the clarinet in the narrow end and put one's hands in two holes and play in the usual manner.

The Forum Cinema opened in 1935. Although built as a cinema, it had a fine stage and was the venue for many stage shows with some of the biggest names in show business. An example was the appearance of a very young Julie Andrews. In later years it developed its own night club called "The Deep". Unfortunately this imposing building was a victim of progress and was replaced with the ubiquitous office block.

One cannot talk about the Forum without mentioning Edward O'Henry. He was the organist who entertained before the start of the films and during the interval. This gentleman was a fine musician and when he died in 1970 he was greatly missed. The Compton organ has survived and is being well cared for.

Jersey Museum Servic

Maurice Harper

This was "The Revellers" at the "Merton Hotel" in 1934. Maurice Harper was on trumpet, "Pansy" Williams (seated) playing tenor saxophone, Syd Britton clarinet and saxophones, Amy Le Gresley piano and piano-accordeon, and Harry Egland drums. Syd Britton's father was responsible for the rather tasteful bandstand covers.

Pip Fairchild

Harold Fairchild, taken in 1936. He was a fine violinist and he was Musical Director at the Opera House. His name can still be seen carved into a beam backstage.

This is Stan Cox and his band at the "Aberfeldy Hotel" in 1935. Stan played alto-saxophone and he is standing on the left of the photograph. Seated next to him is George Woods violin, the drummer is Les Wilford, Harold Johnstone piano and Len Janes clarinet and saxophones. The little man in the front was called Frankie Rowntree; he would do a spot with the accordeon, which is a 48 bass model. The photograph below shows the ballroom at the "Aberfeldy" – imagine sitting around the room waiting to be asked to dance.

David Jo

Author

Len Jar

I could not resist having a photograph of this record. As can be se the recording studio was called "Sound Transcriptions" and address was 25 Seafield Estate, Millbrook. The estate is r Seafield Avenue. Although the record was cut at Seafield Estate, actual recording was made at the Aberfeldy Hotel in 1936. The b was the "Stan Cox Band" and the singer was Len Janes. Len l became the manager of the Aberfeldy until his retirement in nineteen-seventies. He very kindly allowed me to tape this rec and another that was produced at Number 6 Royal Parade, ag about the late 'thirties.

D. Tanguy

The Prince McBride Band at the "West Park Pavilion" in 1936. This is the original line-up with Prince McBride in the right foreground, Julia Harvey piano, Trevor Boston trumpet, 'Dolph McKee tenor saxophone, Douglas Tanguy alto saxophone, Benny Keen drums and Bruce Trent double bass. Bruce left Jersey to seek his fortune and found it when he was discovered by Joe Loss, the famous bandleader; he then went on to become an international star.

R. Britton

"The Saxolean Six" taken in 1936. Jack Dwyer is on alto saxophone, doubling 'cello, 'Dolph McKee is on tenor saxophone, "Dolly" Samson trumpet, Dick Avery banjo, "Pop" de Lavaux piano and Syd Britton drums. When one considers the amount of other instruments on the stand, it makes for a very versatile band. From left to right there are two clarinets, two saxophones, a violin, a soprano saxophone, an accordeon and a 'cello.

G. Arn

G. Arn

Tommy Arnold and his band at the Plaza in 1938. Tommy was a fine exponent of all the saxophones. He played the seasons in Jersey until the outbreak of the war. After serving in the forces he came back to Jersey and played here until his death in 1980.

G. Arnold

G. Arnold

Two novel forms of advertising. The "Plaza Ballroom" was above the "West's Cinema" in Bath Street. The old "Plaza" is no more, having gone the way of so many buildings to make way for the new.

Cyril C. Holt

Cyril C. Holt and his band at the Jubilee Holiday Camp at Plémont in 1938. In later years it was bought by Stan Parkin and later still became "Pontins". It is still "Pontins" today.

This is the Palace Hotel before the German Occupation. It was situated at the top of Mont Millais overlooking St Helier with sea views to the east and west. During the Occupation it was blown up, some say by disaffected German troops. When this photograph was taken, Brian Andrews and his band were playing there.

Auth

Bert Hill

Today this is a bank and a supermarket but in 1939 it was a huge ballroom. It also functioned as a skating rink and in fact was called "The Stadium". After the war it became a cinema with a night club upstairs.

Eddie Tréhiou

Eric Harrison and his band at the New Era in 1939.

CHAPTER THREE

The Occupation

Jersey became occupied by the Germans in the July of 1940. From then on no musicians were coming in or going out of the Island, so in a way it was as if Jersey had been suspended in time. One of the first things that the Germans did was to requisition most of the hotels. Therefore the bands had to turn to the cafés and restaurants, much in the way of the continentals. For the next five years the local musicians had the task of entertaining the people; fortunately we had some very capable people to do so.

On the Classical front, there was P. G. Larbalestier. He had been active before the war with the Jersey Symphony Orchestra and now directed shows like the Grand Opera "Cavalleria Rusticana". He will also be remembered for his composition at the end of the war, "Liberi Gaudeamus".

There was no shortage of talent for the other forms of music. All the various shows had to have music, and this was ably supplied by Jack Coombs, Syd Britton and Cyril Medland. John Blampied formed the "Log Cabin Boys", surely Jersey's first Country anmd Western group!

The most notable change in people's life style was that with the early curfew one could not leave too late to go home, so the obvious answer was to stay the night. This led to some wonderful all-night parties. With a much reduced population there was plenty of room to accommodate everybody.

In the following pages you will meet some of the musicians who performed throughout the Occupation; nobody can thank these people enough for what they did when everything seemed hopeless.

Mrs Becquet

A very popular venue before the war was the "Corner House" in Charing Cross. It was above what is now Senett & Spears. This was the resident band in 1939, "Dusty" Walker's Trio. "Dusty" was the drummer of the band; she was an amazing character. During the German Occupation she was always available to entertain the people, if not on drums then with her comedy routine with a musical saw. Her constant sense of humour helped many people through those dark days. She died in 1987 at the age of eighty-nine.

Eddie Tréhiou

Henri "Pop" de Lavaux band at the "Plaza Ballroom" in 1940. "Pop" is the saxophone player in the centre of the photograph. On his right is future bandleader, young Douglas Tanguy. The pianist on the left of the photograph is Jack Coombs, who produced a number of shows during the Occupation. Trevor Boston is the trumpet player, on his left is Bob Carr alto saxophone, and behind on drums is Benny Keen. The two gentlemen to the right of the photograph are not known. It is interesting that this band had two pianists and the capability of playing three piano-accordeons.

This superb photograph was taken at the "Forum Cinema" in 1942. The Jersey Amateur Variety Band was directed by Reg Perchard. From left to right we have: Stan Perchard banjo, George Ellis mandolin, Reg Perchard mandolin, Raymond Cropp piano, Jack Le Mouton mandolin, Sydney Cavey drums, George Le Gros accordeon, Jack Samson guitar, Harold Bird accordeon, Stan Corfield guitar and John Blampied guitar. This band played all the popular songs of the day. They were later to form the basis for John Blampied's "Log Cabin Boys". In the foreground can be seen the Compton organ. The story goes that a wooden case, with a large padlock, was built to protect the organ. A German officer wanted to play the organ but naturally nobody knew where the key was, so he disposed of the lock with his pistol and proceeded to give a brilliant performance to his small but enthralled audience.

Stan Corfie

What a contrast to the former photograph of the Forum stage. This is the German Luftwaffe band in concert at the Forum in July 1942. They were conducted by Stabs-musicmeister Steinbach.

A. May

Eddie Tréhiou

Here we have a photograph of that fine drummer Ernie Lamy, taken whilst practising at the Plaza Ballroom in 1940. During the Occupation Ernie lived in Cannon Street and of course, as there was no motor transport, it must have been a sight to see Ernie trundling his drums along the street to the Plaza. Towards the latter part of the war Ernie had a motor-bike accident and was told that he would never leave his bed. This courageous man not only proved them wrong but played trumpet with various bands for many years.

L. Le Marinel

Elsewhere in this book I mentioned the high standard of musicianship enjoyed by the Salvation Army. This is not surprising when one considers this photograph. Here are three generations of musical talent. Les Le Marinel is the youngster, his father in the middle and his grandfather on the right. All three rose up through the ranks to become bandmasters, and many people will remember Les when he was bandmaster of the Band of the Island of Jersey. This photograph was taken in 1942. Note Grandfather's long service medal with bars.

This superb photograph was taken at the "Plaza Ballroom" in 1943. The "Plaza" was situated above the "West's Cinema" in Bath Street; sadly it was knocked down to make a shopping precinct. What is so special about Occupation period photographs is that cameras were banned. The only photographs permitted were in a studio setting, and even then the material was censored. This band of lovely ladies was called "The Melody Girls". From the left of the photograph were: Jeanne Labesse piano, Peggy Hawkins violin, Edith Isherwood accordeon, Barbara Berry drums, Peggy Le Caudey accordeon and Solange Labesse 'cello. The band was put together by "Dixie" Landick and Graeme Ahier and performed light popular music of the day. The microphone would be a collector's item today.

Dixie Land

During the Occupation John Blampied formed the "Log Cabin Boys". One might say they were the first Country and Western band in Jersey. Here is one of the "Boys", Edouard Tréhiou, taken at a studio in 1944.

A. I

ILLIS ELLIS

Mrs Richardson

MABEL SLADE

Mrs Richardson

In 1944 the Dramatic Section of the Green Room Club presented their most ambitious programme, a night of Grand Opera. Here we have the ladies who performed that Easter. In the "Cavalleria Rusticana" were "Lucia" played by Phillis Ellis, "Santuzza" by Beryl Jordan and "Lola" by Mazel Slade. The Musical Director was P. G. Larbalestier and the Producer Max Le Feuvre. The Opera House was the venue and it proved to be a fantastic success.

RYL JORDAN

Mrs Richardson

OPERA HOUSE

(Manager: A. V. FRASER)

Week commencing Easter Monday, April 10th,
Nightly at 6.30 p.m., with Matinees on Thursday, April 13th
and Saturday, April 15th at 2.30 p.m.

The Dramatic Section of the
Green Room Club (Founded 1909)
presents
for the first time in the history of the Club
a programme of

Grand Opera

"Cavalleria Rusticana" ... *Mascagni*
"Faust" Act III .... *Gounod*
"Il Trovatore" Act IV Scene I *Verdi*

Musical Director.... Mr. P. G. LARBALESTIER
Producer .... Mr. MAX LE FEUVRE

PROGRAMME - - - THREEPENCE

Filleul & Queen, Printers

The original programme for "Cavalleria Rusticana", April 10th, 1944. This Grand Opera proved to be a huge success

Here is John Blampied leading his band in 1945. During the Occupation John was responsible for creating the "Log Cabin Boys". In this photograph John is playing guitar, Doug Le Caudey is on saxophone, his brother Jeff on drums, and Ernie Lamy trumpet. The venue is thought to be the "Anneport Bay Hotel". That speaker cabinet must be a collector's item today, and what about the amplifier under the piano?

Eddie Tréh

When the Islands were liberated there was a great demand for bands. Musicians had more work than they could cope with. During 1945 a lot of the hotels that had been taken over by the Germans were opening once more. Mainland musicians had not yet started to arrive and so the local musicians had to try and cope. This was a popular band of the day. John Blampied piano, Edouard Tréhiou accordeon, Bert Hill violin and Mick Honeycomb drums. The venue was "La Mare Du Mont" which later became "Bal Tabarin" and later still "Adrian's".

Eddie Tréh

CHAPTER FOUR

Jazz and the Big Bands

The nineteen-fifties started with the established bands playing at venues like the "West Park Pavilion" (now "Inn on the Park"), "The Plaza" and "The Rainbow Room". Apart from these, small bands were to be found at many of the smaller hotels. Without exception the musicians were turning more and more to jazz. This was the time of Count Basie for the big bands, and Dave Brubeck and Oscar Peterson for the small bands. It went a long way to explaining the improvement amongst musicians of improvisation and technique.

The Jersey Musical Union was going strong and was much in demand. Classical music was being served by the newly-formed Jersey Arts Council.

It was at this time that the Modern Music Club was formed, later to become the Jersey Jazz Club.

Tourism was getting back on its feet. Floorshows and cabarets were becoming popular forms of entertainment. "Tams Pantry" was perhaps the best of these. The "Opera House", "The Little Theatre" and the "Forum" were all putting on shows, and hotels like the "Merton" and "Hotel l'Hermitage" were catering for the honeymoon trade. Even the Salvation Army brought over some of their British bands and, as always, they were excellent.

So the music scene was set. One may be forgiven for thinking that there was no need for change, but across the Atlantic there was a Country singer called Bill Haley who was playing something completely different.

Stan Corfield

Here we have the Les Watson band the "West Park Pavilion" in 1947. L is the clarinet player at the right of t photograph, next to him is tenor sax phone player Brian Andrews, behir him is Les's brother Ted on trump Denis Riley is the alto saxophonist the centre of the photograph, t drummer is Art Castle (he drown at St Brelade's Bay whilst trying rescue a holidaymaker), next to h is Roy McKee, the piano player Douglas Appleby, and at the micr phone is vocalist Stan Corfield.

JEP

This unusual photograph was take in 1947 when the Band of the Roy Militia Island of Jersey were hande back their instruments which ha been carefully hidden from th Germans throughout the war by J. I Le Breton. Mr Le Breton is the gentl man third from the left. Far left is Bi Rattenbury, next to him Colon Vatcher, then Mr Le Breton, Henr Grube, Mac(?) and Ernie Free. What collector's item the van would b today. Mr Le Breton was awarded th British Empire Medal for his wo during the Occupation.

Ken Pleece

Another of the smaller bands was at the Merton Hotel. This is the Clem Randolf Band in the summer of 1949. Clem is on drums, Charlie Morse saxophone and clarinet, Johnny Bowery on piano, and Ken Pleece doubling saxophone and double bass. Note the interesting microphone.

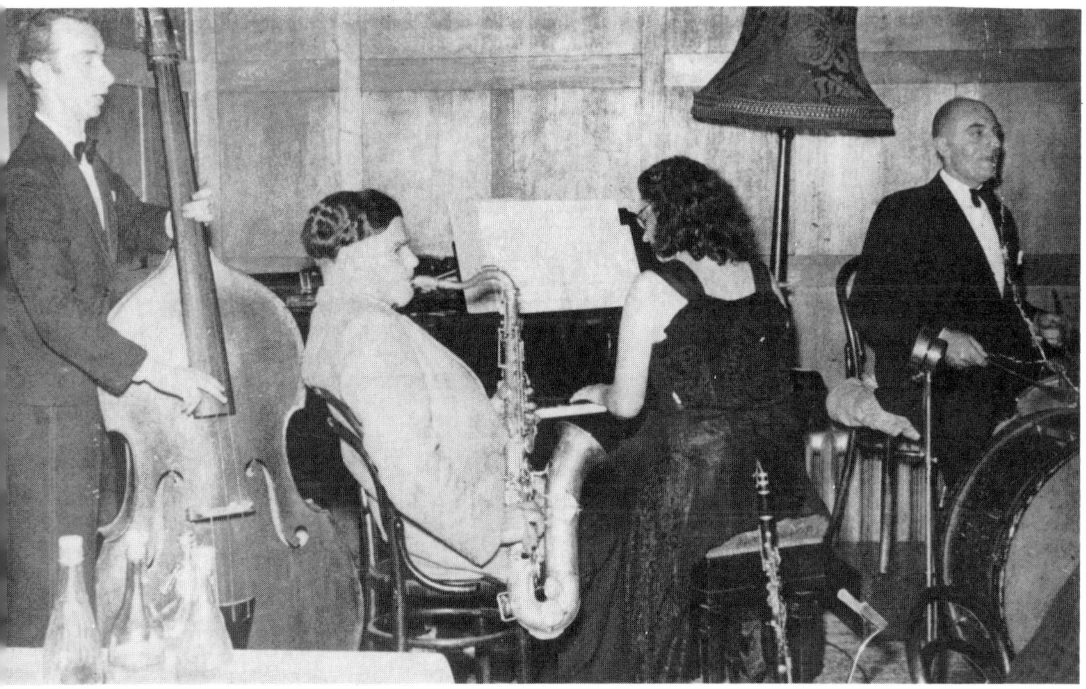

Kenny Lane

Dance bands were in great demand during the late 1940s. The big bands were at places like "West Park Pavilion" and the "Plaza" but there were small bands at the smaller hotels. This quartette played at a St Brelade hotel in 1948/49. Charlie Scott is the saxophone player, with Marjorie Ahier on piano, Kenny Lane bass and Harry Egland drums.

Here we have the Trevor Tanton band at the "New Era" ballroom in 1949. Trevor is the alto saxophone player in the centre of the photograph, next to him on tenor saxophone is Bud Howdon. I understand that Bud was the joker of the outfit, sometimes clanging a large bell in the middle of a romantic waltz. On Bud's right is Roy Murphy on alto saxophone, Harold Wheeler is the pianist, a young Jack Lamy on bass, and Bill Gorman on drums.

Roy Murp

So popular was dance music that it was even possible to fill a parish hall. This is the Bert Hill trio playing at St Ouen's Parish Hall, Christmas 1951. Apart from Bert on accordeon, there is Rosa Beakbaine on piano and George Morris on drums. What a fine Christmas tree tucked in the corner.

Bert

Kenny Lane

In 1954 the Jersey Modern Music Club was formed. Here we have a typical line-up at the "Plaza" with Denis Riley on alto saxophone, Brian Andrews tenor saxophone, Stuart Woolstone piano, Kenny Lane bass and Johnny Taylor drums. Stuart Woolstone and Kenny Lane were the originators of the club. In the following year this nucleus of musicians, along with Ray Kitchen, formed the Jersey Jazz Club.

This is the "Hotel l'Horizon" band in 1955. Richard Ames was the bandleader, seen here with the violin, Ken Ward piano, Hal Blinston bass, and Alan Rich drums. They were the resident band for four years.

Hal Blins

This is the Jack Rede Trio at "La Tonnelle" Lounge in 1955. The "La Tonnelle" was in the old "St Helier House Hotel" which is now known as "The Imperial Hotel", La Motte Street. Jack is on drums, and fronting the band is that great baritone saxophone player Buddy Featherstonehauge. I heard Buddy play at the Jazz Club at the Rainbow Room, Georgetown, and I have never forgotten what a wonderful experience that was. He played two seasons in Jersey before moving on.

Joe P

Norman Jones

This is a typical line-up for a dance band in the mid 'fifties. In the top photograph is Johnny Van Derek on violin, Bill Page piano, Johnny Crawford bass, and Norman Jones drums. The other photograph shows Johnny Van Derek on trumpet, an instrument he played as well as the violin. This time Reg Cranmer is on piano, Bill Winnie on bass and again Norman Jones on drums. The venue is the "Continental". All these men were fine musicians but unfortunately not always appreciated. It was Bill Winnie who, when asked by a rather snooty lady, "Mr Bass Man, can you play some Rock and Roll?" replied "Madam, we are ****ing musicians". Bill had learnt his profession with the London Symphony Orchestra.

Norman Jones

The Norman Jones band at the "Continental" c.1955.

This photograph taken in 1954 shows an excellent line-up of saxes. Denis Riley is on the left on baritone, then Eric Harrison tenor, Dick Charles tenor, unknown and Brian Andrews. The rhythm section is Stuart Woolstone piano, Kenny Lane bass and Johnny Taylor drums.

Dennis Ri

The "Ray Kirkwood Trio" at the "Hotel de l'Europe" in 1955. Ray is the guitarist. For some years after he left, Ray was looking for a summer season in Jersey but the musical climate changed and as time went by there was less chance of him coming over. The pianist is Bill Matthews; like most pianists of the day he would double on accordeon. Many people will recognise a young Ray Kitchen on drums.

Ray Kitc

Ray Kitchen

This is a fascinating and rare photograph. It is the "Jersey Jazz Club" the year it was formed, 1955. It was at the "Rainbow Room" above the "New Era", Georgetown. Denny Brown is the saxophone player, the pianist is Stuart Woolstone and the drummer Bobby Adrian. At that time every hotel had a band and there were many fine jazz musicians in Jersey. Two of these are the unnamed trumpet player and the guitarist who was called Larry. He was with Ben Johnson's "Caribbean Heatwave" which was the summer show at the "Rainbow Room". Many of the people who went to the Jersey Jazz Club will remember Denis Coffey, seen here on bass. A terrific band.

Kenny Lane

This is Bruce Trent at the "West Park Pavilion" in the mid-1950s. Bruce was a local boy who left Jersey to find fame and fortune, and found both when he became an international recording star. He took the name from Lady Trent who inspired him to rise to the top of his profession.

CHAPTER FIVE

Rock and Roll

Although it was not obvious at the time, 1956 was to change the accepted form of music for all time. In America, Bill Haley and the Comets had recorded "Rock Around The Clock" and a young man called Elvis Presley was making a name for himself. Closer to home, Lonnie Donnegan had a hit with "Rock Island Line": his form of music became known as "Skiffle".

It was late in 1956 that Jersey's first "Pop" group was formed. They were called "Hank Terry and the Mainliners" and were a Country and Western group. A change of musical direction came with skiffle music, and that is what the group became noted for. It was not long before other groups were formed, all playing skiffle, the culmination of which was a skiffle contest at the "West Park Pavilion" in 1958.

It was, however, "Rock and Roll" which was to dominate the music scene for the next few years. Late in 1958 the first rock and roll band in Jersey was formed. They were called "The Five Aces". I can remember the older generation complaining that the group was too loud and that they could not understand the words, but this was a young person's music. It was new, it was exciting and it set the trend for all that was to follow.

Meanwhile other forms of music were still being played. Dance band trios and quartettes abounded, but change was in the air, and the groups were starting to play in the venues which had traditionally had bands. Jazz was still drawing the crowds; in fact it was at this time that the Jersey Jazz Club came into its own. Military and Brass bands were as popular as ever, but a sad event was the closing of "The Little Theatre". The "St Cecilia Orchestra" played the last concert there in February 1959.

It is hard to believe the radical changes that would occur in the next thirty years, and this was the beginning.

thor

In November 1956 "Hank Terry and the Mainliners" was formed. This was the first "group" in Jersey. They played Country and Western music, at a time when few people had heard any. The group featured a steel guitar, played by sliding a bar of steel along the strings to give it that distinctive sound. Terry Bourke sang lead vocal and played guitar, Chas Larbalestier vocal and guitar, Cyril Lewis steel guitar, and Dave Bourke double bass. The group became so popular that they performed on radio and television both locally and nationally.

Ray Kitc

This is an interesting photograph for a number of reasons. First of all the venue was the "Olwyn Grove Hotel", one of the first hotels to fall victim to apartment conversion. This photograph was in 1957/58. Secondly, Denny Brown is playing clarinet and he was mostly seen with his tenor saxophone. Stuart Woolstone is on piano, Ron Chance bass, and Ray Kitchen drums. It was Stuart Woolstone and Ray Kitchen who formed the Jersey Jazz Club in 1955, at the "Rainbow Room" above the "New Era Cinema".

Kenny L

This is the Art Mauger Quartette at the "Sunshine Hotel" in 1958. Art is the alto saxophone player, Eric Tricot on piano, Kenny Lane bass, and Dick Le Claire drums. Although the band played mainly for dancing, like most bands at this time they were strongly influenced by jazz – for example the music of Oscar Peterson, Stan Getz, etc.

Wally Adams

In 1958 a young man would go to the Rainbow Room dance hall at Georgetown and ask if he could sing with the Nat Gonella band. It just happened that a duo calling themselves "The Avons" went to hear the band and were so impressed with Ray Adams that they asked him if he would be interested in joining them. For Ray it was a dream come true. In November of 1958 they recorded "Seven Little Girls Sitting in the Back Seat" which went to number three in the "Pop" charts.

Eve Bouchet

Auth

M. Carré

Dave Whitfc

When "Skiffle" music became popular a number of groups were formed. In 1958 there was a skiffle contest at "West Park Pavilion". This was the group that won. Called "The Rockislanders", they were a six-piece band. Leon Bouchet took lead vocal and played rhythm guitar, Glyn Edmonston vocal and guitar, Maurice Beward vocal and guitar, Tony Percy washboard, Peter Fitchet T-chest bass, and Harry Gould drums. Here we see them performing at the "Seaforth Hotel".

This rare photograph was actually taken the night of the skiffle contest at the "West Park Pavilion" in 1958. The group was the "Silk Cuts" and they came third. Tony Bertrand was the lead vocalist, Dave Baudin rhythm guitar. An unusual feature was Mo Carré on accordeon. Brian Le Flock was on T-chest bass and Pat Allenet on drums.

The "Black Diamonds" were sec in the 1958 skiffle contest. T photograph was taken in 1958 on "Forum" cinema stage. Chas Lar estier is the main vocalist, Tre Beaton vocal and rhythm gui George Lane lead guitar, Ron Bou bass, and Clive Isaacs drums.

Another of the young groups in skiffle contest was "The Hotspots" unusual feature at that time beir female vocalist. Ivy Hamon was singer and played rhythm gui Other guitarists were Colin Whitf and Ken Snell, Ted O'Donag played T-chest bass, and Da Whitford drums. Here they performing at the "Marina Ho L'Etacq, in 1958.

Author

The first Rock and Roll band in Jersey. "The Five Aces" consisted of Tony Bertrand vocal and rhythm guitar, Mick Walsh lead guitar, on double bass Tod O'Donaghue, Norman Vautier bass guitar, and Denis Ollivro drums. This is the band on stage at the "West Park Pavilion" in the autumn of 1958.

M. Kavanagh

In 1960 a party of "Rockers" was invited to take part in a "Rock and Roll" contest in Guernsey. Here they are at rehearsal with the popular "Five Aces" providing the music.

This was a good band. Denis Riley on saxophone, Mary Taylor vibraphones, Eric Taylor piano, and Stan Corfield on drums. The venue was the "Grand Hotel" in 1959.

Denis R

Here is the "Pomme d'Or" band in 1959. Jock Reed saxophone, Bob Brookes piano, Johnny Linker bass, and Johnny Taylor drums. Most interesting decor. Bob Brookes was featured in the first Channel Television programme in the September of 1962.

R. Broo

JEP

"Hank Terry and the Mainliners" at the BBC studio in Manchester, celebrating their part in winning the "Top Town" television competition in 1959. The group sang the song "Teeny Weeny Bikini" which explains the scantily clad Astrid Hyde-Clark.

One of the best singers on the cabaret circuit in the late 'fifties/early 'sixties was beautiful Peggy Ray. Peggy has retired from the profession but she is not forgotten by many people who had the pleasure to work with her. A very nice lady!

Dick F

CHAPTER SIX

The Swinging Sixties

As far as music in Jersey was concerned, the 'sixties started rather quietly. The dance bands were still in demand, and the Rock and Roll bands were only doing a short spot, almost like a cabaret. Elvis Presley, Cliff Richard and the Shadows, and the Everly Brothers were the most popular artistes for the first three years. Locally "The Aces","The Crescendoes" and "The Meteors" were rocking them in the aisles. It was at this time that a few of the youngsters got together and formed the "Whitfield Jive Club" at the "Rainbow Room". This was a huge success, people queueing all the way up the road for a chance to get in. Many were disappointed, as there was a limit to how many the place could hold.

It was not long before another venue was started. This was at the "West's Plaza Ballroom". Both "The Aces" and a new group, "The Cousins", were to be found there. Meanwhile, "The Meteors" were doing youth clubs and church halls, until at last they started playing regularly at the "Prince of Wales", Greve de Lecq. One must remember, this was young people's music, and with it went the mini-skirt and bee-hive hair-do for the girls, and Elvis Presley haircuts for the boys.

Later in the decade, of course, there was "The Beatles". They had rather a hard time when they came to Jersey and played at Springfield, but in late 1963 they went to number four with "She Loves You". It was a bad blow to the established bands. For the next three years the bands who could not, or would not, adapt to the new style of music fell by the wayside. It was the young who dictated what they wanted to hear and dance to, and this has continued to this day.

It was perhaps as a reaction to this that in the late 'sixties Jazz, Country and especially Folk music came to the fore. Jazz people were fortunate to have musicians like Jack Duff and Gary Lloyd to promote the music wherever they could. Country music had always been played, but now there were established bands like "The Country Gentlemen" and the "Tennessee Three".

But it was the Folk scene that really took off. First-class entertainers like Gerry Lockran, Dave Head, Johnny Silvo, plus all the resident Folk people, were to be found at Tony and Nim Baal's Jersey Folk Club, Mike Harris and Ernie Roscouet's Folk Club, and the Ritz Folk Club. Music was very much alive and well.

"Johnny Cook and the La Moye Five" at the "La Moye Hotel" in 1960. Johnny is the drummer in this photograph, Denis Riley is blowing baritone sax, Vic Carter tenor sax, Maurice King guitar and Hal Blinston bass guitar (one was more used to Hal with a stand-up bass). This was a popular and well-liked dance band at the time.

Denis R

Jack Rede's trio at the Chelsea Hotel in 1961. Fronting the band is Marcel Sanson – he was a champion accordeonist from France. Tony Aked is the pianist and Jack is on drums.

Jack R

Author

Author

In 1961 "The Aces" had reached their zenith. Everybody wanted to book this Rock and Roll band; they were playing West Park Pavilion, the Plaza and the Whitfield Club at the Rainbow Room. Tony King was the lead vocalist, with Mo Whitford on lead guitar, Ken Snell rhythm guitar, Chas Larbalestier bass and Denis Ollivro drums. The lower photograph shows Josie Andrews fronting "The Aces" at West Park Pavilion.

"The Cousins" in action at the Grève de Lecq Pavilion in 1962. Tony Bertrand is the vocalist and played rhythm guitar, Mick Walsh lead guitar, Ken Thomson bass, and Barry Walsh drums. Some years later the Pavilion was burnt to the ground and when rebuilt called "Caesar's Palace".

Au

One of the Rock and Roll bands in 1962 were "The Meteors". At this time John Manning was the lead vocalist, Pete Michel lead guitar, Martyn Michel guitar, Bob Michel bass, and Gerry Harrington drums. Later Gerry became a very successful Disc Jockey until his departure for Australia. Many will remember this group when they played at the "Prince of Wales" Hotel, Greve de Lecq.

John Mann

By 1963 Rock and Roll was changing to a heavier format. The Beatles and the Rolling Stones had changed the face of music for all time, and Great Britain dominated the music charts. Jazz was still proving popular but one had to know where to go to hear it. As always the Jersey Musical Union were still in demand, but their days were numbered. The Royal Jersey Light Infantry Band was still active, but it too was soon to come to an end. Both these bands were to come together as the "Band of the Island of Jersey", and that is what they are today.

Folk music was set to take off. In the latter part of the 'sixties Ricky Hudson and Gerry Jackson were working hard to produce their style of Folk, encouraging a lot of the local artists to appear instead of singing and playing at home. Traditional Jazz was finding favour with a new breed of enthusiasts, whilst there were concerts for the lovers of Classical Music. Dance bands were still in demand but they were having to update their material. Country Music was having one of its periodical revivals. In general there was music in Jersey to suit everybody. On the Rock scene "The Heartbeats", "Cair Paraval" and many other groups were providing "Beatles" orientated music, but the music was changing. Groups like "Pontiac", "Soho Sect" and "People's People" were presenting covers of "The Kinks", "Fleetwood Mac" and "Simon and Garfunkle".

There was also a tendency for groups to do their own material. It was not easy to persuade people to accept this, but there were some up and coming writers in the Island, and they were to become better known in the 'seventies.

Here are "The Crescendoes" in 1962 at the West Park Pavilion. The group consisted of George Staff lead vocalist and rhythm guitar (George had played with Joe Brown and the Bruvvers), on lead guitar was "Diz" De Ste Croix, Paul Wroe-Johnson bass, and Mo Ollivro drums. This group was to become the longest enduring band in Jersey; as musical taste varied, so did their material, but always to a very high standard. On more than one occasion they were asked to play in the U.S.A. and Europe but they had no need to leave Jersey to show their talent.

Mo Olliv

One of the later Rock and Roll bands to emerge was "The Hearbeats". Here we see them in action at a club dance in 1963. Wendy Heritage and John Manning are sharing the lead vocal, Basil Le Riche is on lead guitar, Pete Hilditch bass, and Gerry Harrington drums.

John Mann

Pete Double

The "Perido Four" at the Pomme d'Or Hotel in 1965. This band played a mixture of Pop Music, Jazz and Swing. Pete Double fronted the band on clarinet, with Mick Carrel on guitar, Phil Adams bass, and Jim Burt on drums. They were the resident band for many years at the "Hotel de l'Europe".

D. Crafter

What makes this an unusual trio is that there were two guitarists. On the left of the photograph is Maurice King, the other guitarist is Des Crafter, and Marty Huet is in the centre on drums. This was at the "Stable Bar", Hotel Angleterre, in 1964. Marty Huet later played for Country band "The Country Gentlemen".

Hal Blinston

In the early nineteen sixties there was still plenty of work for small trios and quartettes. Here is a typical dance band of the period at the Norfolk Hotel in Colomberie. Mary Taylor is the pianist, Hal Blinston bass and Derek Jones drums.

C. Coo

One of the many groups of the middle 'sixties was "The Argonauts". The line-up was Leon Channing on lead guitar, Clive Cooper rhythm guitar, Alan Hall bass, and a hairy Steve Querée on drums. Clive was not a great guitarist, but many will vouch for his ability to play keyboards. It was in fact this ability that enabled him to start his music shop "Easy Play Studios". One cannot help but admire Steve's drums, and Leon's guitar would be in demand today.

Pat Coll

This is a group from the mid 'sixties, "The Pat Collins Combo". Pat is at top right and played guitar, top left is Buddy Bisson drums, next on the right is bass player Mike Harris, opposite him Mo Horsborough keyboards, bottom right singer Stan James, and left Ron Wiess flute. Although they played for dancing, they tended to entertain people in the style of a showband.

Les Falle

This was the "Soho Sect" at Springfield in the summer of 1966. Derek "Griff" Griffin was the lead vocalist, Leon Channing lead guitar, Mervin Watkins vocal and rhythm guitar, Peter Ward bass and Les Falle drums. There is an interesting selection of guitars here, with Leon's Fender Jaguar, Merv's Gibson and Peter's Hofner bass.

JEP

Here we have "People's People" at the "Tropicana" in 1966/67. Colin Alner was on lead guitar, Bob Frampton vocal and guitar, "Lummy" bass, and Rob Whitbread drums. "People's People" first came to Jersey to do a one-off gig and proved so popular that they had to return.

N. M. Ca

Jersey has had many stars of international fame, both performing and relaxing, but not many have actually lived and worked here. "Yana" was the exception. This lovely lady came to our shores in the 'sixties, fell in love with the Island and made it her home. Her last show in Jersey was in 1975 when she had her own show at the "Blue Fox". Although so well known as a singer, she also had been an actress in films and on the stage. "Yana" passed on in 1989; I hope this will serve as a small tribute to "The Lady".

JEP

It must be said that the musicians in 1967 were an intrepid bunch. The swinging pianist is John Blampied; he could always be relied on if one wanted to do something a little bit different. Along with Mo Horsborough accordeon, Mike Fosse saxophone and Richard English drums, they all set off for the Chausey Isles to do a gig. Unfortunately the piano fell off the truck that was taking it to the venue. After major surgery it was restored to playable condition and a good time was had by all.

JEP

Billed as "Richard and Nola" this duo performed a variety of music. Nola sung and accompanied herself on the guitar and Richard filled in with brilliant guitar backing, as well as playing superb Flamenco and Classical pieces. Richard must be one of the few guitarists in the world to go and teach Flamenco guitar in Spain. Here they are in 1968 when they were resident duo at "The Old Court House", St Aubin, later to become famous as "The Royal Barge" in the BBC programme "Bergerac".

Ernie Roscouet

On the right is the man who has done more than anybody to promote Folk Music in Jersey. Ernie Roscouet, along with Mick Harris, started the Jersey Folk Club in 1968. They brought to Jersey some of the most well-known Folk artists of the day. Some of them stayed and played seasons in Jersey, and here we have two of them. On the left is Dave Head and next to him Johnny Silvo. Here the trio are performing at the Ritz Hotel.

This was a very talented band, well named "The Sophisticats". Although they were a dance band, these musicians were second to none, as proved by the many years they played at the Woodville Hotel. They liked nothing better than to be asked to play a Jazz standard so that they could display their skill. Here we see them in action in 1968. Gary Lloyd is on organ, Johnny Lowe bass (and tamborin) and Dave Harris drums. Dave had replaced Keith Chalkley on drums.

This was the "Gary Bond Combo" in July 1967. Gary is the organist, Cyril Lewis on steel guitar, Pete Hilditch bass and Kenny Snell drums. Not long after this photograph was taken Gary took his combo to India to take up a position as resident band. Cyril Lewis stayed in Jersey to form his own band. Gary replaced Cyril with guitarist Mick Walsh and they left for India. Some may remember that bass player Pete had previously played with "The Heartbeats", Kenny Snell had been with "The Aces" and Cyril Lewis was steel guitarist with "Hank Terry and the Mainliners" with Gary on drums.

Ernie Roscouet

Gerry Lockran in 1967. Gerry was a fine blues singer and he had a very distinctive style of guitar picking. He was at the Caribbean Bar, Hotel de la Plage. Gerry was asked to record a session for Channel Television and it is sometimes re-shown and is well worth watching. Everyone was shocked by his untimely death in 1987.

Chris Bellée

John "Pix" Pickford (everyone knows him as "Pix") came to prominence in the late nineteen sixties as a superb singer and guitarist. In fact in 1968 he won the *Jersey Evening Post* popularity poll as the best individual singer. Since then he has played in every major Rock band in Jersey. He became best known as the founder-member of the "O Band".

The "Jim Henry Trio" at the Chelsea Hotel in 1967. This was the year they were voted the band of the year in the *Jersey Evening Post* popularity poll. Jim is on guitar, Ronnie Beckford on piano and Dave Louis on drums.

Jim He

I could not resist this excellent photograph of Jack Duff with Benny Waters, taken at the Opera House in 1968. Benny was one of the first American musicians to come to Jersey and he was considered by some to be the finest saxophone player in the world.

Jack D

Les Falle

This was "Cair Paravel" as they appeared in 1967, just prior to leaving these shores to seek their fortune. Derek Griffin (Griff) was the singer, a dynamic performer who could be relied upon to excite and win over even the toughest audience. The lead guitarist was the clever Basil Le Riche (his Gibson "Les Paul" guitar had the most amazing action). Val Risdon was on bass and Les Falle drums. Here they are at Lords nightclub.

Mo Ollivro

Here are "The Crescendoes" at "The Deep" in 1969. They were a much larger and a much different group to when they had first started back in the early 'sixties. The front man was Steve Huelin vocal and guitar, with Wally Langley trumpet, Pierro Guido saxophone, Pete Michel lead guitar, Paul Wroe-Johnson bass and Mo Ollivro drums.

J. Stopher

"National Steam Union" – N.S.U. as they became known – were a young band in their early 'teens. They were formed in 1969. Terry Quinn was the lead singer, Jeff Jackson lead guitar, Steve Moss rhythm guitar, John King bass and John Stopher drums. They played a mixture of music but were heavily influenced by the "Rolling Stones". It is interesting to note that the venues where they played, like "The Place" (Little Theatre, Providence Street) and Grève de Lecq Pavilion (Caesar's Palace), are no longer there.

This terrific photograph was taken at the 1969 Battle of Flowers. On the top of the fire-engine is trumpet player Johnny Begley, Tony Parr is next to him (also on trumpet), Johnny Taylor has brought along his bongo drums, and behind him is Jack Duff on soprano saxophone.

Jack Du

"Mo's Mood", the new-style dance band of the late nineteen sixties. The emphasis was on multi-vocal harmony with a strong driving rhythm. This was ably supplied by Mo Horsborough on keyboards, the prominent bass of Bob Michel, and the crisp drumming of Brian Bradley. Mo went on to become a very popular solo artiste in the 'seventies at Swanson's Hotel, and many people will remember his accomplished accordeon playing. The guest singer in this photograph is Kenny Jenkins, who sung in the style of Billy Eckstine.

David Hole

n De Cruchy

Ron De Gruchy was the guiding light behind the "Sound Set". Ron played keyboard, Barry Maclachlan (Mac) guitar and bass, and Bob Harrigan drums. Here they are at the Hotel Angleterre during their 1969 season. They were one of the few bands to adapt to the changing face of music; strong vocals and a driving rhythm kept their audiences on the dance floor.

CHAPTER SEVEN

Towards a Wider Audience

If it can be said that there was a high point for music in Jersey, the early 'seventies was that time. This was the time of long hair, flared trousers and flower power. For the lovers of Rock, one of the places to go was the "Underground" at the Demi des Pas Hotel. There you could listen and dance to "Parlour Band". Modern Jazz was being ably supplied by Jack Duff and his merry men, whilst Jazz of the more traditional sort came from "The Treasure Island Jazz Band". At the Royal Hotel, people who liked Country Music were being catered for by "The Country Gentlemen" where the "Silver Dollar Country and Western Club" was held. Folk Music was having one of its rounds of popularity with people like Johnny Silvo, Dave Head and many others. Nearly every good hotel had a trio or quartette playing mainly for dancing. Syd Lawrence and his band were as popular as they had always been.

For the lover of brass bands, one could hear the "Band of the Island of Jersey" in the Howard Davis Park, as well as at various fêtes throughout the summer. There was music for everybody's taste. This situation continued for some years, but towards the latter part of the 'seventies things were changing. Gradually musicians were finding it more difficult to find places to play. Many of the venues were adapting to a disco situation. Towards the end of the decade music in Jersey was at a low ebb.

Jim Hall

n Pleece

Traditional Jazz has always been a popular form of music and when the "Treasure Island Jazz Band" was formed they were an instant success. In this photograph are two of the band, Ken Pleece on banjo and Bobby Shannon on drums. Ken will always be a bit special to me because it was when I met him in March 1987 that he suggested I write a book about music in Jersey.

Pete Double

Here are the rest of the "Treasure Island Jazz Band". On clarinet is Derek Riseborough, John Pashley is on cornet, Graham Mosely trombone and James Hall on bass. The photographs were taken during a "gig" at the Bath Hotel in 1970.

This photograph will bring back memories of when Ray Kitchen had his music shop in York Street. The photograph was taken in 1970. The three heroes struggling with the organ are Clive Cooper (nearest the van), Ray Kitchen (centre) and Bill Bean (on the left). It looks like they are trying to put a quart into a pint pot.

W. Be

One of the most popular music shops in Jersey was "Arkay Sound". This is the studio section of the York Street shop. It belonged to Ray Kitchen , a man who devoted his life to music, both as a working musician and as a supplier of musical instruments and accessories. Here is Ray on the left of the photograph, with drummer Johnny Cook centre and Rob Le Sueur, guitarist, on the right. As often happened with Ray's enterprises, there was often a glass to celebrate something. This photograph was taken in 1963. Nobody has to be told that Ray has a very successful business these days, in his Bath Street shop.

Ray Kitch

Author

Pete Balcam and Ernie Roscouet at the Royal Hotel in 1971. Pete was an exponent of the "Ragtime" guitar which complimented Ernie's folk style vocal.

Rick Hudson

During the early 'seventies there was a great interest in Folk music. Here is Ricky Hudson at a concert in 1970. Ricky and Gerry Jackson brought over most of the better Folk artistes at that time, first at the Caesarea Hotel, then to the Ritz Hotel, and for some years at the Royal Hotel. Ricky is noted for his individual style of performance, which includes the faintest touch of satirical comedy.

"The Travellers" were a Folk group formed in 1971. Sadie Le Sueur provided the lead vocal, Ernie Roscouet vocal and guitar, and Phil Adams was on bass.

Ernie Rosco

This is Mick Harris performing at the Royal Hotel in 1971. Mick, along with Ernie Roscouet, was the founder of the Jersey Folk Club in 1968. Here he is being backed by "The Country Gentlemen".

Author

When the great Ella Fitzgerald heard Molly Anson she said: "If she looks as good as she sings, she must be very beautiful." This is the beautiful Molly performing in 1971. Jack Duff is on clarinet and Gerry Rossi on bass.

Pete Balc

:. Anders

This was the "Parlour Band" when they were formed in 1971. The line-up was Peter Filleul on keyboards, "Pix" Pickford guitar, Craig Anders guitar, Mark Anders bass and Jerry Robins drums. The band was formed by Peter Filleul who was able to gather some of the best musicians in Jersey to play his sort of music. They played solid Rock, but what made them so different was their ability to produce excellent vocals with a strong element of harmony. Here they are photographed in Peter's grandmother's parlour, hence the name of the band. Not long after this they recorded "Is A Friend?" for Decca, one of the few Jersey bands to interest a major record company.

Pete Balcam

This is the basic "Parlour Band" at the "Underground", Demi des Pas Hotel, in 1971. Craig Anders, Mark Anders and Jerry Robins are part of the original group with the addition of Jon Grove guitar, Bernie Ward tenor and baritone saxophones, and Pierro Guidi on tenor saxophone. It was a little later than this photograph that the "Parlour Band" with original members "Pix" Pickford and Peter Filleul made their LP for Decca.

Pete Balcam

Jerry Robins with "Parlour Band" at the Demi's "Underground" in 1971.

That very popular duo Mick and Fran Clinton at a Jersey Folk festival in 1971.

Pete Balca

Christmas charity appeal in the Royal Square in 1971. This is John Duthiel shortly before he left for Australia. John's hobby was flying falcons.

Pete Balcam

Colin Alner

When Colin Alner first came to Jersey with his group "People's People", Christmas 1966, little did he realise that he would return and make Jersey his home. In 1972 he formed that very popular group called "The Electrums" who played a mixture of Rock music and Pop covers. Here we have Roy Hollis in the centre (he was the lead singer and played rhythm guitar), Colin on the right of the photograph played lead guitar and occasional vocal, Sid Smith on the left bass, and Rob Le Quelenec drums. They were the regular band at Sands night club, Five Mile Road, for four years before finding other outlets for their talents.

David Hole

This is the "Simon Raverne Sound" at Les Arches Hotel in 1972. Simon takes the lead vocal and plays both rhythm and lead guitar, "Taffy" Edwards is on bass and Eddie Thorpe drums. This very popular trio played a mixture of Rock and Roll and Country Music.

Jack D

Jack Duff, A.T.C.L., is probably the best known musician in Jersey. He has been a keen promotor of Jazz in the Island for many years but he has always taken time out to listen to every sort of music and contribute to it if he was able. Here he is with his band at the old "Tropicana" in 1971. Mike Capocci is on piano and Gerry Rossi on bass, out of picture is Roy Tomlinson, drums. This was the band that, with that great trumpet player Kenny Wheeler, made the LP "The Enchanted Isle" in 1971.

Jack D

Local musicians with personnel from the Syd Lawrence Band. Johnny Begley is on the left, holding the trumpet, Eric Ashworth is in the centre smiling benignly, next to him looking like one of the Mafia is "Pip" Fairchild, on his left is Al Cornish, Mike Harris is on his haunches looking very brown, and on his left is Stan Martin. The photograph was taken at "Cliff's" Bar.

Ray Kitchen

"Fogg" consisted of a variety of musicians with a similar feel for the music they wanted to play. An unusual feature of this band was that they used two drummers. In this photograph there is: bottom centre Ken Snell drums, on his left Brian Skelley drums, on Ken's right Brian Noel guitar; in the centre Steve Howard vocal and guitar, on his left Robin King saxophone, behind Steve on his right is John King bass; back left, Mick Crawford flute and Miney Rye keyboards; top right is Colin Gully, roadie. This was the line-up in 1972. Sometimes there were personnel changes but this was the band called "Fogg".

JEP

This is "Lynn and the Midnight Sun" at the Continental Hotel in 1971. What a shame we do not have many bands like this one in Jersey. They were the resident band for about a year at the "Conti". For the people who are interested, the stack behind Lynn was all Binson equipment.

J. Stopher

This was "Shaggrat" in 1973. Taking the lead vocal was Alex Johnson, Leon Channing lead guitar and bass, Brian Noël lead guitar, Roger Norman keyboards, and John Stopher drums. One of the first gigs for this band was the Peter Parker Appeal Fund at the New Plaza Ballroom. Heavy Rock was the order of the day. It would be fair to say that "Shaggrat" were the first Jersey-based band to present a visual aspect to their performance.

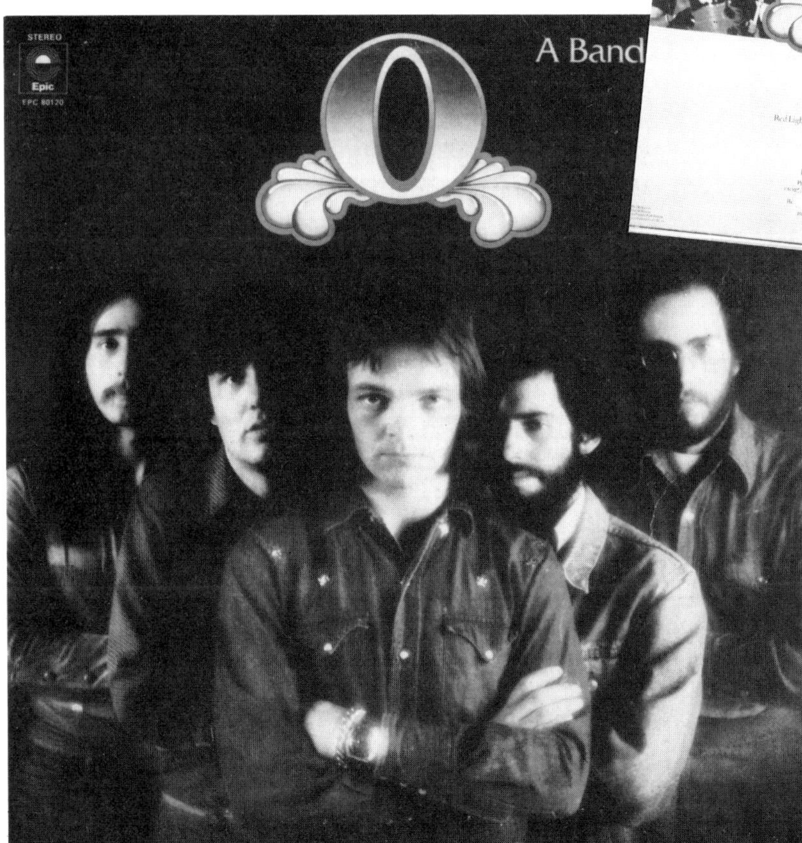

D. Calbeldu

This was "A Band Called O" in 1974. What a wealth of talent in this group. If circumstances had been different, this band would have been up there with the greatest. John "Pix" Pickford was the lead singer and played fine guitar, Craig Anders lead guitar, Peter Filleul keyboards, Mark Anders bass and Derek Ballard drums.

Pete Balcam

A typical dance trio of the early 'seventies, the "Mary Carlisle Trio". Mary is on piano, Jim Hall bass and Dick Le Claire on drums. 1972.

Ron Keen

Although dance band music was not as popular as in previous years, La Moye Hotel continued to have dances into the early 'seventies. In fact even today they cater for dancing functions. This is a selection of good musicians doing a "gig" there in 1972. That grand old man of the saxophone, Tommy Arnold, is fronting the band, Ron Keen is on guitar, that excellent pianist Bert Messeder is on piano, his son André on bass and "Honky" Hall is on drums. André left Jersey to take up an appointment as a bass player on the ship Queen Elizabeth.

"The Country Gentlemen" as they appeared in 1974. Here they are performing at the "Les Charrières Hotel". Lew Milne was the singer and played rhythm guitar, Cyril Lewis steel guitar, and Martin Huet drums. They had been formed to be the resident band at the "Silver Dollar Country Music Club", and when the club closed its doors, they carried on.

Phyllis H

This is a part of the Norman Allen Showband. This excellent and entertaining band was the resident band at the Hotel de France in 1973. Norman was the drummer, pictured here with his wife June as lead vocalist. On the right is his keyboard player. The rest of the band consisted of guitar, bass and saxophones.

J

Mike Hanigan

This very popular duo were formed in 1975. Mike Hannigan took the lead vocal and played excellent rhythm guitar, Brian Noël sung harmony, played lead guitar breaks and did the musical arrangements. The duo were strongly influenced by the music of Simon and Garfunkle, Crosby Stills and Nash and their own original material.

C. Cooper

For many years "Three's Company" were the resident band at the "West Hill Country Club". Here they are c.1976. Clive Cooper played keyboards, Ray Garwood bass and Ray Valerio drums. It is interesting that a three-piece band could still be in such demand at this time when many hotels were employing disc jockeys.

Auth

This is the "Les Copley Trio" taken at "The Tavern", Hotel de France, in 1975. This was an excellent band and played for some years on the band circuit. Only the death of "Little Les", the band-leader and drummer, ended this very popular trio. James Coates was the pianist and Mick Harris was on bass.

D. Craf

Although most of the hotels and dance halls were using disc jockeys in 1979, there was still the odd dinner and dance that would hire a trio for the evening. They may not play together on a regular basis, but would form for the gig. Here we have Leni Reed on piano, Des Crafter guitar and Paul Cockerham drums. The venue was the "Greve d'Azette Hotel".

Jack Duff

Trumpeter Johnny Begley and veteran clarinet player Doug Tanguy having a "Jam" session at the West Park Pavilion in 1977. It is interesting that Douglas had been blowing for more than forty years when this photograph was taken. (See plate 29)

Cyril Holt

This is the "Cyril C. Holt Trio" at the Royal Hotel in 1978. Cyril is fronting the band on saxophone, Bert Messeder is on piano and Tommy Cunliff drums. By the late 'seventies "gigs" were becoming hard to find.

In 1978 "Memory Lane" entered and won the competition "Search for a Star". As a direct result they appeared on national TV in the programme "Seaside Special". At that time the group consisted of Norman Clarke lead vocal and rhythm guitar, Paul Denton vocal and lead guitar, Chris de Gruchy bass and Tom Jordan drums. All the boys sung harmony which was well suited to their 'sixties type of music. In 1979 they released an LP record called "Souvenir".

Ann and Keith Seym

This is the group "Shady Lady" in 1975/76. The photograph epitomises the aggresive attitude that was to find expression in Rock music during the late 'seventies and throughout the 'eighties. Keith Curtis is seated on the right of the photograph (he played lead guitar), next to him is Terry Quinn main vocalist and keyboard player, John Stopher drummer, and John Cox bass. The venue is "Scarlet's" at L'Auberge du Nord.

J. Stop

Sandy Gold

"Sandy Gold" at the "Sunshine Hotel" in 1979. This vivacious performer helped put on a show that was seen by many thousands of holiday makers. Sadly "Sandy" is not working as much as she used to, not having the time to devote to her first love, which is singing.

G. Hayman

Gary Hayman at the piano at "Swansons Hotel" in 1975. Although very well known as a solo pianist, Gary has been involved with bands and groups, that is apart from writing music and promotional work. As if that was not enough, he also finds time to teach music.

CHAPTER EIGHT

Music, Music Everywhere

The nineteen eighties saw a marked improvement in the music scene in Jersey. Many of the hotels were employing dance bands: for example, "Victoria's" at the Grand Hotel, "Hotel l'Horizon" etc.

It was in the early 'eighties that the "Black Butter Jazz Band" came to prominence: they could be found at the Pomme d'Or Hotel on Sunday nights. In 1982 the "Marlboro Country Music Club" opened its doors at the "Wolf's Caves". "The Barnstormers" were seen regularly on Channel Television, whilst at La Moye Hotel there was the "Nashville Country Music Club".

It was during the middle of the decade that Jack Duff organised the "Jersey Big Band" and they could be found on a Sunday morning at the Opera House bar. Apart from that, Jack was running his own band and promoting Jazz wherever anybody was prepared to go and listen.

Young musicians were making their presence felt. Bands like "The Boogie Brothers", "Pressure Point" and "Two Minutes Mister Smith" were playing a wide variety of music for the younger people. What is interesting was that they were as popular as the ubiquitous D.J. For the Heavy Rock fan there was "Outlaw", "Hunt the Dark Night" and "Women and Wyne".

Les Falle started his Rock and Roll revival nights for charity, at Springfield. Using bands from the 'sixties with D.J.s between the groups, the evenings were a great success.

Some of the credit for musical awareness in youngsters must go to the Education Committee. They encouraged music at Highlands College, employing some of the best teachers it was possible to get. These hard working teachers also toured the schools and it was not long before there was the "Le Rocquier Band". Under the watchful eye of Mel Davidson and his team, a "Jersey Youth Orchestra" was formed and then a "Jersey Youth Wind Band". "La Ronde Concert Band" was next, and they were able to pick the best of both the young and the not so young musicians. The most impressive event was the forming of the "Jersey Symphony Orchestra". There had not been a full blown orchestra for many years, and this one certainly made up for it.

The Folk Clubs were doing well. At the "Smugglers' Inn" on a Sunday night could be found many of the Folk lovers, or on a Tuesday or Thursday at the "Devil's Hole" and "Royal Hotel".

W. Bean

This is Bill Bean's trio at the Ommeroo Hotel in 1980. People may remember Bill when he had the group called "The Prime". Here he has Tony Spence on bass and Bobby Shannon on drums. Although Bill is still available, Tony went to Australia and Bobby now lives in England. It is an interesting point that so many of our musicians have left Jersey to seek their fortunes in Australia.

E. Roscouet

This is the "Black Butter Jazz Band" back in 1981 when they played for the Heart Foundation Ball at St Ouens Manor. Pete Double is in the foreground on clarinet, to his right is Andy Thomson Trumpet, on bass is Colin Lilly, Ernie Roscouet guitar and Les Campion drums. Black butter is a local product made with apples, mixed with molasses and spices. The whole is stirred continuously for twenty-four hours non-stop, and the end result is a substance not unlike jam.

The "Barnstormers" were formed in 1983 when they answered a request for a band to play for a square dance. The band continued to perform this type of music, but they found that they were often being asked to play Country Music standards and they were soon playing regularly. Because of this popularity, they were approached by Channel Television and completed a long series of programmes for them. Johnny Mason is the lead vocalist, Chas Larbalestier plays lead guitar, Colin Goss steel guitar, Dianne Larbalestier bass and Steve Querée drums.

Auth

In 1982 the Marlboro Country Music Club opened its doors. This club has gone from strength to strength at its venue in Wolf's Caves, St John. The band that has been with them from the beginning is "Country Mood". Apart from some changes in personnel this excellent band has proved to be very popular, both with the local members and the many visitors to the club. In this photograph we have Brian Mooney on the right (he is the lead vocalist and plays guitar, mandoline and ukelele), seated at the piano is Mick Maguire (vocal and keyboards), Keith Pike is the bass player, and "Pip" Fairchild drums. Apart from playing their regular sessions they have been supporting band for many of the Country artistes that have come over.

Ted Lawren

Liz Keeler

Ceilidh bands are popular wherever they appear. The Caesarean Ceilidh Band is no exception and here they are at the Royal Hotel, David Place, in 1985. Since then there have been some changes in personnel but they have managed to maintain the essence of the band.

Norman Hilton

The resident band at the Hotel l'Horizon in 1983. Pete Thompson is on saxophone, Norman Hilton piano, Eric Ashworth bass and "Honky" Hall drums. "Honky" played for the Teddy Foster Band back in the 1950s, a household name to British big band fans.

Dick R.

Stuart Gillies, a fine singer, was to be heard at Caesar's Palace, Greve de Lecq. This photo was taken during the 1984 season. Although Stuart is a Scotsman, he has long been part of the Jersey musical scene, and as such is considered an honorary Jerseyman. He has had many successful seasons in Jersey over the years. In 1972 his record "Amanda" went to No. 8 in the charts which assured him international stardom, and he is still in great demand world-wide for cabaret appearances. But Jersey is still where his heart (and home) is.

Robbie Alexander

Jennie Jensen

Extreme left:
This is Robbie Alexander. He played as a professional entertainer all over Europe before returning to Jersey to settle down. He continues to have the same success since his return.

Left:
In 1986 Jennie Jensen was invited to appear at the "Best of British" Silk Cut Country Music festival at Wembley. Jennie was "on the road" for many years before returning to her native Island.

M. Hannigan

One tends to think of concerts in the park as the perogative of military and brass bands. This photograph shows that it is not always so. "Thin On The Ground" appeared at the People's Park in 1985. Mike Hannigan is in the centre of the picture, Mike took the lead vocal and played guitar, Dave Cabeldu on the right, vocal and lead guitar. On bass was Paul Machon and Barney Johnson percussion. This "gig" proved to be extremely popular, perhaps someday it can be repeated.

N. Clarke

A very different "Memory Lane" from the group that won "Search for a Star" back in the late 'seventies. Here they are at a charity performance at "Swansons Hotel" in 1986. The boys all sing, both individually and in harmony. They are noted for their arrangements of music of the 'sixties.

The group called "Pressure Point" were formed in 1985. Here they are at the "Skyline Disco", Hotel de France. This was a very popular band and they were support band for some of the big names that came to places like the Gloucester Hall, Fort Regent. Keith took the lead vocals, with Simon on keyboards and Nigel guitar. Later they were joined by Suzanne on saxophone adding a little glamour to the line-up. Another welcome addition was Wayne on drums, making this a formidable outfit.

Simon

One of Les Falle's Charity Rock and Roll revival nights at Springfield Hall in 1985. The group is "Pix and Friends" assembled specially for the occasion. In this photograph "Ferret" is fronting the band, on the right is "Pix", Keith is on the left of the photograph on lead guitar, with the two Johns on bass and drums respectively. Les has raised thousands of pounds for charity and all of the leading musicians and disc jockeys have performed in them at one time or another.

J. Stopher

JEP

JEP

Robin McEwan conducting the Jersey Symphony Orchestra at their inaugural concert in December 1986. Martin Marsay is the Leader.

A section of the Jersey Symphony Orchestra at their unaugural concert in 1986.

JEP

At this concert in 1987 at the Art Centre, Dawn Daghorn flautist and Stuart Hepburn guitarist were given a chance to show their collective ability. Also taking part in the concert was pianist Miles Clery Fox.

The "Tennessee Three" taken at Swansons Hotel, Esplanade, in 1987. Terry Bourke is in the centre, and he takes the lead vocal and plays rhythm guitar. Chas Larbalestier sings harmony and plays lead guitar, and David Bourke sings harmony and plays bass.

Auth

Gerry Jackson in 1987. Gerry has been on the Jersey Folk scene for many years; in fact he was one of the performers at the Jersey Folk Festival in 1971. In 1987 he was the chairman of the newly-named Jersey International Festival of Traditional Music, Song and Dance.

JEP

This was Tony King and the "Kings of the Road" at the La Moye Hotel in 1987. They were the resident band at the "Nashville Country Music Club".

Bob Michel

Chris Voisin

Here is "Katch" in the early nineteen eighties. This capable and very popular band were resident as Les Arches Nightclub for almost three years, having previously played successful seasons at The Blue Fox and Kontiki Nightclubs. Their "clean cut" image was unusual for bands at that time. The members are, from left to right: Jeff Hathaway guitar and vocals, Peter North lead guitar, Pete Brookes keyboards and vocals, "Digs" Le Long drums and vocals, and Chris Voisin bass and vocals.

Roger Bara

A name synonymous with the Jersey music scene in the 'eighties, Roger Bara has been Musical Director at Caesar's Palace nightspot since 1982, with "The Roger Bara Band" earning several Variety Club "Best Band" Awards. Roger has also been M.D. for the long-running Jersey Green Room Club pantomime since 1985. On the recording side, he has produced over 40 albums, the majority of which he has arranged, orchestrated and performed himself, as well as having written numerous published jingles, themes and library packages in his own studio, "Music Workshop".

The young band "Sons of Fascination" had an excellent year in 1987. Early in the year they were runners-up in the T.S.B. Rockschool Competition, they appeared with Alison Moyet, and they took part in the tape "Class of '87". This is apart from working at the various nightspots.

In August of 1987 there was a Rock Jamboree at the "Barge Aground" at St Ouen. Eight local bands took part, one of which was "Two Dogs At It". Here they are in action, as always never boring.

JEP

The Jack Duff Quartet at the Jersey Jazz Festival in March 1988. Here they are with Alan Randall guesting on vibes. Jack is fronting the band on alto saxophone, Mick Carrel on guitar, Gerry Rossi bass and "Pip" Fairchild on drums.

Author

Bob and Sue Beslièvre made up the duo called "Twice As Nice". Here they are performing at the "Le Coie Hotel" in 1988. In the background, beating the tamborin, is Pete Webb, entertainment manager for the hotel. Some people may remember Pete in the 'sixties as guitarist for the duo "Webb and Wayne".

"Outlaw" is the group that won the Benson & Hedges Rock contest in March 1988. They went on to be the supporting band for "Marillion" when they appeared at Fort Regent. Tony Kempster plays guitar, Steve Baudins guitar, Craig Belliard guitar, Simon Roberts bass and Jason Smith drums.

"Exile", one of the runners-up in the Benson & Hedges Rock contest. The competition was held in March 1988.

JEP

This is the Jersey Big Band at the "Inn on the Park" in November 1988. The occasion was a Tea Dance for anyone who could remember how to dance.

JEP

In 1988 it was decided to have a Tea Dance at the "Inn on the Park", using the Jersey Big Band to provide the music. This is the saxophone section taken on that occasion.

One of the Rock bands in 1988 was "Joe Public". This was the line-up that played at the "Blue Fox" nightclub.

One of the young Rock bands in 1988 was "Women and Wyne". They consisted of Dennis O'Driscoll lead vocalist, Tracy Smale harmony vocals, Jason Hingston lead guitar, Warren Lynham bass, Gary Reid vocals and keyboard, and Neil Hingston drums. This very young band will provide some of the musicians of the future – they play hard and loud, but have all the enthusiasm of youth.

JEP

This young Rock band won the 1988 Channel Islands Rock contest. A capacity crowd were at the "Lido de France" to cheer the bands on. Mark Law was the lead vocalist, ably backed by Andrew Chatterley on keyboards, Neil Guégan drums and Peter Vautier bass. With young bands like this one coming to the fore, there should be no worries about the future of music in Jersey.

JEP

Another of the Rock bands of 1988 was "Songvolution". This band had an unusual approach for a young band in that part of their appeal was their visual image. Patrick Sheill was lead vocalist and lead guitarist, with the added bonus of being able to write new material, William Smith keyboard, Danny Lloyd bass and James Bell drums. It says a lot for this band that they were able to stand next to experienced musicians during a Rock and Roll revival night and hold their own.

Musicians are often asked to do something for charity and they are only too willing to oblige. This group of fine musicians was no exception. The group was called "The Recorder Consort" and here they are in March 1988. From left to right are Philippa Le Feuvre, Robin McEwan, Helen Brooks and Stephanie Shifrin.

George Villiers in 1988. George is a true aristocrat, in the nicest sense of the word. Viscount Villiers lives and performs with his new ensemble in England but his home is Jersey. He plays some of the compositions that he has written but he will play anything that he feels contributes to the style of his ensemble.

La Ronde Concert Band was formed in 1982. What started as an experiment developed into an enthusiastic collection of musicians from various backgrounds. Here they are at rehearsal in 1985 under the conductorship of Brian Frost.

This is the bubbly "Diane Cousins" as she appeared at "Caesar's Palace" nightclub in 1988. A very popular lady, people would go to see her year after year.

Dick Ray

Stan James was a drummer in the nineteen sixties, a singer/guitarist in the 'seventies, and a fine solo vocalist in the 'eighties. What people do not know is that Stan is a prolific song-writer. This talented man has worked with some of the most respected musicians in Jersey, and on the occasions when he has worked out of the Island he has stood alongside some of the biggest names in show business. This is Stan taken during the 1987 season.

Stan James

Dave Wright

This is "Two Minutes Mr Smith". Here they are in 1989 at the "Blue Fox" nightclub. The basic band stayed the same, but any musicians were made welcome if they wanted to sit in.

W. Jennings

"Two's Country" – Mandy and Bill Jennings – as they appeared at "Wolf's Caves" for the 1989 season. Their style of Country music proved very popular with both the local people and the holiday-makers.

This is Robert Tilling. He is head of art at Victoria College in Jersey as well as being a very fine individual working artist. This photograph was taken of Bob just before the 1989 First National Blues Festival to be held at Burnley at Easter. Bob is to MC the festival and give a lecture and demonstration. The guitar is a 1935 National guitar, made in America, and what makes it interesting is the large metal plate on the front. This acts as a sound box, much in the way of the soundbox on the old wind-up gramophone. Bob usually picks the strings but occasionally he will use a "bottle neck" to achieve a slide effect. In fact many of the steel guitarists use their guitars as a second acoustic instrument.

There is no doubt that Colin Amos, the band-leader of the Le Rocquier Band, was a proud man when they won an audition to play at Disney-world, U.S.A., early in 1990. Here, they were presented with a cheque to help finance the trip.

CHAPTER NINE

Now and The Future

By the end of the nineteen eighties every type of music was being well catered for. The most promising areas were the youngsters graduating from Highlands College and going to music colleges in the United Kingdom, and the progress made by youth clubs and the Education Department to encourage youngsters in every form of music, not least the fine recording studio that was set up with the help of Marc Daghorn.

A number of Rock bands that became established in the nineteen eighties were still playing, although often with different personnel.

The Jersey Symphony Orchestra was kept very busy, now performing regular concerts annually. These were very popular and well attended.

Jazz continued to flourish, especially with the annual Jazz festival. These occurred early in the year, just before Easter, and continued to attract more and more people each year.

Country Music continued to be popular during the 'eighties, certainly enough to support two clubs, open throughout the winter, and a number of additional venues throughout the summer.

The Folk scene was perhaps where the biggest growth occurred. Some of the people who had performed during the mid 'sixties and early 'seventies were coming back to the clubs and showing what they could do.

The Jersey Big Band was expanding its horizons by playing at other venues. They were also proving that there was still a call for ballroom dancing.

In 1989 one of our local lads won a gold medal for shooting at the Commonwealth Games; the band played what some regard as Jersey's National Anthem, "Ma Normandie". This caused some controversy within the Island, and it was suggested that "Beautiful Jersey" may be more appropriate.

Whatever your taste, Jersey does have a lot to offer as we go into the nineteen nineties.

Acknowledgements

Acknowledgement has been individually given to all the photographs in this book, but I would like to thank the following for additional help and advice: Robin Briault, Roy Moore, Helier Vibert, David Jones, Michael Richardson, Jan Nash (JEP), Mrs Le Cornu, George Drew, Eddie and George Arnold, Joe Pinto, Ian Montins, Mrs Becquet, Mr N. Carne, Anita and Richard Mayne, Mrs Le Provost, Mr Lamerton, Mrs McLinton, Marion Bickerton, Mrs De Tolède, Mr Coutanch, Andrew Millar-Dick, Sue Hardy, Ron Doublet, Don Le Boutillier, Reg Queree and the staff of the Public Library.